LEARN TO DRAW

VILLAINS

LEARN TO DRAW

Disney

VILLAINS

Walter Foster
Jr.

TABLE OF CONTENTS

Tools and Materials

You'll need only a few supplies to begin drawing. You may prefer working with a drawing pencil to begin with, and it's always a good idea to have a pencil sharpener and an eraser nearby. When you've finished drawing, you can add color with felt-tip markers, colored pencils, or even paint. The choice is yours!

drawing pencil and paper

eraser

sharpener

colored pencils

felt-tip markers

paintbrushes & paints

HOW TO USE THIS BOOK

In this book, you'll learn to draw all of your favorite villains in just a few simple steps. You'll also get lots of helpful tips and techniques to help guide you through the drawing process. With a little practice, you'll soon be producing drawings of your own!

1 First draw the basic shapes using light lines that will be easy to erase.

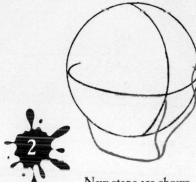

2 New steps are shown in blue, so you'll know what to draw next.

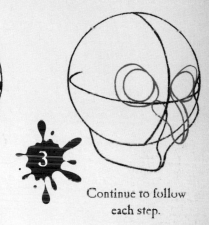

3 Continue to follow each step.

4 Draw in the details.

5 Darken the lines you want to keep, and erase the rest.

6 Use some villainous magic (or crayons or markers) to color your drawing!

DRAWING EXERCISES

Warm up your hand by drawing squiggles and shapes on a piece of scrap paper.

Draw a square

Draw an oval

Draw a circle

Draw a rectangle

Draw a triangle

Circle

Ball

Triangle

Ice cream cone

Pizza

Sun

Square

Gift

House

Rectangle

Book

Balloon

Oval

Submarine

Truck

INTRODUCTION

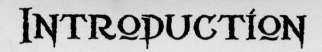

In every Disney and Disney/Pixar movie, loathsome villains will try every evil trick in the book to defeat and conquer the heroes we all know and love. From Scar's malicious attempts to overthrow Simba and Cruella De Vil's malevolent obsession with Dalmatian fur to the ill intents of Captain Hook, Jafar, and Ursula, each Disney villain has his or her own story to tell. Fortunately for Peter Pan, Aladdin, Ariel, and our other favorite heroes, the good guys always win. But that doesn't mean that you can't enjoy learning to draw the infamous foes you love to hate!

What makes a Disney villain so memorably malicious? It starts with a simple shape, followed by the fine details, such as the dagger-like eyes of *Sleeping Beauty's* powerful fairy, Maleficent; Captain Hook's moustache that twitches with every tick-tock of the crocodile's clock; or the arched brows and blood-red lips of Ariel's nemesis, Ursula, in *The Little Mermaid*. These are the types of details that characterize the infamous Disney villains, revealing dark characters who frighten and threaten to destroy those who dare to oppose them.

Many Disney villains are intimidating because of their clothing, as well. From Cruella De Vil's stark black-and-white fur wardrobe to Jafar's scarlet-red cape, a villain's colors are always bold, dark, and foreboding. By combining sharp edges and billowy layers, these villains appear larger than life!

Villains also come in all shapes and sizes. Consider the tall, bumbling Stabbington Brothers from *Tangled* or the thin, lanky, voodoo-wielding Dr. Facilier from *The Princess and the Frog*. Short and stout defines smart-mouthed Iago from *Aladdin*, while the louder-mouthed

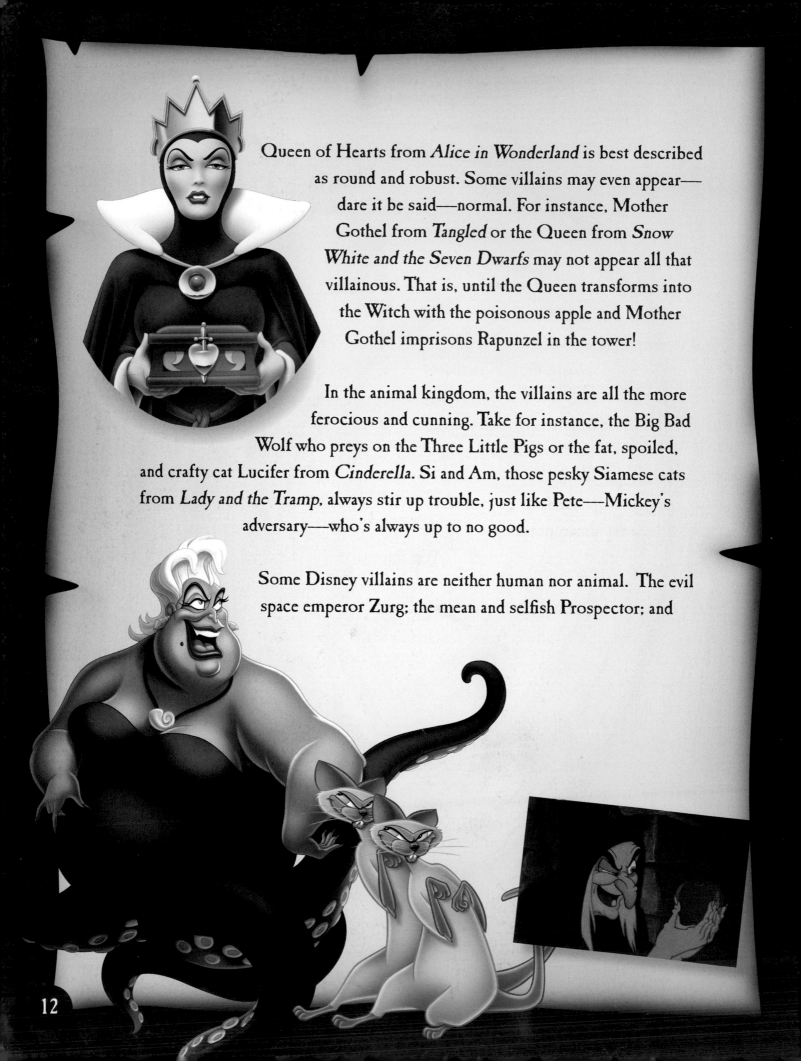

Queen of Hearts from *Alice in Wonderland* is best described as round and robust. Some villains may even appear—dare it be said—normal. For instance, Mother Gothel from *Tangled* or the Queen from *Snow White and the Seven Dwarfs* may not appear all that villainous. That is, until the Queen transforms into the Witch with the poisonous apple and Mother Gothel imprisons Rapunzel in the tower!

In the animal kingdom, the villains are all the more ferocious and cunning. Take for instance, the Big Bad Wolf who preys on the Three Little Pigs or the fat, spoiled, and crafty cat Lucifer from *Cinderella*. Si and Am, those pesky Siamese cats from *Lady and the Tramp*, always stir up trouble, just like Pete—Mickey's adversary—who's always up to no good.

Some Disney villains are neither human nor animal. The evil space emperor Zurg; the mean and selfish Prospector; and

Lotso, a completely un-huggable strawberry-scented teddy bear—all from the *Toy Story* movies—prove that villainous tendencies aren't limited to people. And Chick, Professor Z, Grem, Acer, and Miles Axlerod from *Cars* and *Cars 2*, as well as Autopilot and GO-4 from *WALL-E*, show that villains can even take the form of automobiles and robots.

So now that you are familiar with these infamous Disney villains, it's time for you to take up your pencil and learn to draw them! Simply follow the step-by-step instructions, and you will see how wonderfully talented you are as you draw the evil villains from all of your favorite Disney and Disney/Pixar movies.

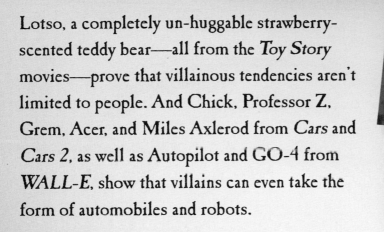

PETE

Pete is never up to any good—his only goal is to aggravate Mickey Mouse and his friends. So make this guy appear as menacing as ever. Start by drawing a circle for his head. Add a pear-like shape for his body; then fill in his large, round legs and arms and other details.

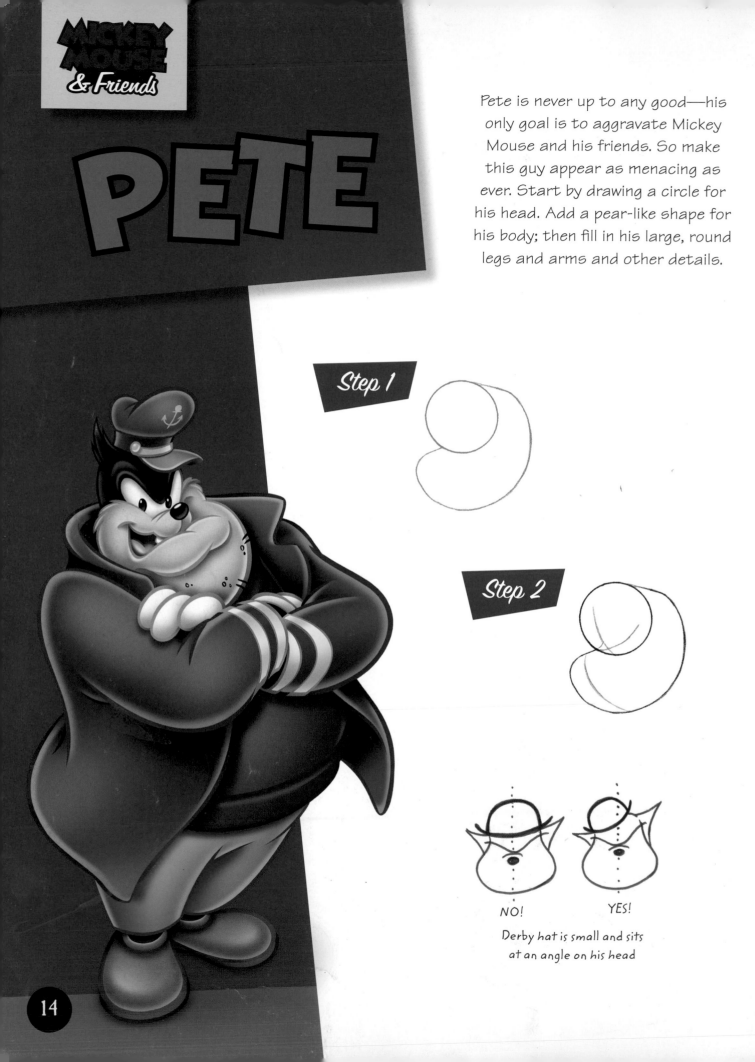

Step 1

Step 2

NO!   YES!

Derby hat is small and sits at an angle on his head

Step 3

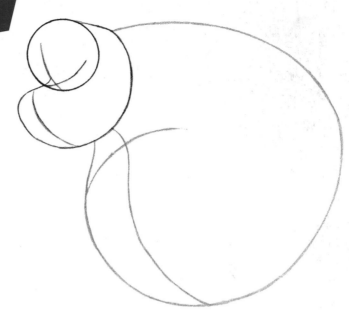

Step 4

YES!

NO!

brows are thick and
bushy with uneven ends

Step 6

vest is old
and tattered

Once you've finished your drawing, give Pete some color. Maybe then he won't look so mean— or maybe he'll look meaner.

Step 7

CAPTAIN HOOK

Captain Hook is no longer sailing the seas looking for treasure as a fearsome pirate. Instead, he's hunting down Peter Pan, and he won't stop until he has revenge! Although he lost his hand, Captain Hook is still a skilled swordsman, ready to duel with Peter Pan every chance he gets.

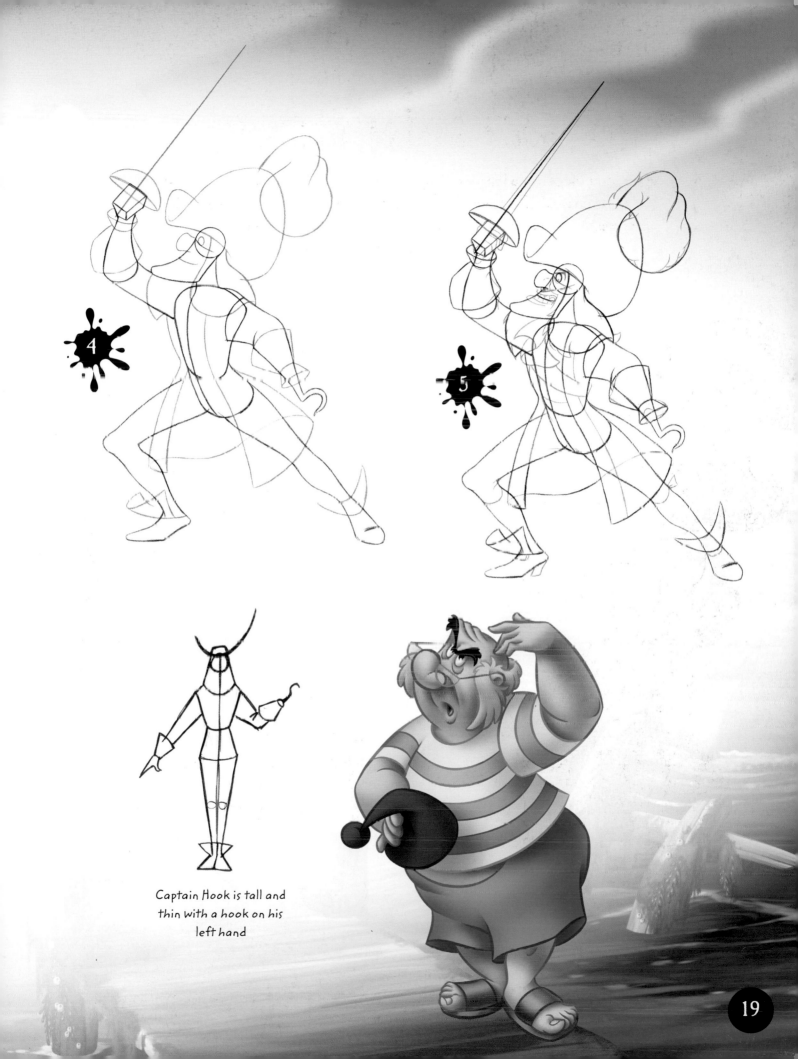

4

5

Captain Hook is tall and
thin with a hook on his
left hand

moustache is
symmetrical with
very long ends

6

shape of hat is uneven;
the plume comes out
of the center crown

Si and Am

This destructive duo is always looking to cause trouble.
Si and Am are sneaky villains who love to get into mischief
and then let others take the blame. Don't forget to include
their crooked tails and exposed teeth.

Cat head starts
with an oval

Dog head starts
with a circle

Si and Am have three whiskers
on each side of the face

4

Nothing amuses this duo more
than seeing Lady in trouble

Note the angle for the
placement of the eyes,
which will help create
their expressions

5

MALEFICENT

Maleficent is the most powerful fairy in the land. She embodies pure wickedness, and she even refers to herself as "the mistress of all evil." The folds of her robe trail behind her, so make sure to capture that detail in your drawing.

1

2

3

She wears a large black ring
on her right index finger

She has a long narrow body;
the flowing sleeves on each
side represent flames

4

head is symmetrical; note the three angles to the horns on her headdress

Color Maleficent's skin green and give her cheeks an appropriate tinge of rouge for depth and detail

5

THE BIG BAD WOLF

As you draw the Big Bad Wolf, keep in mind all the little details you need to add: his claws, his teeth, the tattered hem of his trousers, and the wrinkles in his snout. Make sure you get every bit right...otherwise, he'll huff, and puff, and blow your house down!

1

2

YES!

Top hat is old
and worn

NO!

Hat doesn't
look new

YES!

NO!

only one suspender
holds up his pants

While the Big Bad Wolf looks ferocious, hungry, and unforgiving, he still hasn't caught the Three Little Pigs

6

Tail comes out of a patch in the back of his pants

Queen of Hearts

The Queen of Hearts always looks aggravated, annoyed, and just plain mad. If she's not yelling "Off with their heads," she is playing a frustrating game of croquet. She is a larger-than-life villain wearing a tiny crown. As you draw her, try to keep her proportions intact.

Earring detail

She carries a large heart-shaped fan

2

3

This villain's name may be the
Queen of Hearts, but she certainly
doesn't have a heart of her own—
that we know of

1/4

1/2

The ends of the underskirt
detail touch the bottom and
the top fourth of the dress

torso is a large heart shape over a full, bell-like skirt

There is an overskirt on top of the underskirt

Lucifer

Lucifer is a truly devilish cat—and the favorite pet of Cinderella's evil stepmother, Lady Tremaine. He may be a fat cat, but he loves chasing mice and causing loads of trouble for Cinderella. As you draw Lucifer, keep his nails sharp, his eyes watchful, and his tail fluffy.

4

Lucifer has a large grin with lots of sharp teeth

Lucifer's smile doesn't hide the
evil that's inside

eyes are slanted to give him a
sly expression

YES!

Nose is oval,
not round

NO!

Cruella De Vil

Cruella De Vil is obsessed with fur coats. So much so, that she steals Dalmatian puppies for their fur so she can make one. It doesn't get more evil than that! She has a striking profile, with a slender frame, pronounced jaw, and eyes full of menace.

Hair is black on her right side and white on her left side

2

3

Cruella wears a large green ring on the index finger of her right hand

4

she wears long red
opera gloves

face resembles
a skull

5

URSULA'S HEAD

This view of Ursula's head shows the depth of her full face.
The flame-like shape of her hair frames her face and suggests her evil mind.

Although Ursula's head is small, her jawline is very wide. Angular ovals create her eyes and eyebrows

4

5

6

Don't forget Ursula's "beauty" mark

Ursula's Body

Ursula is constructed of simple shapes. Her six legs can be used either to propel her or to act as extra arms. All six are not always visible.

6

legs should appear to join
together underneath
Ursula's wide body

7

URSULA'S BODY

Ursula manipulates everyone to get what she wants. She is selfish (not shellfish) and even though she steals Ariel's voice, she never steals the song in Ariel's heart.

Ursula has six tentacles (or "legs") instead of eight

Detail of her
shell earrings

Detail on shell
around her neck

6

Ursula has three eyelashes on the top lid and two on the bottom

brows have a high arch; they are thicker in the center and taper to a point

URSULA'S EXPRESSIONS

Ursula's gestures and expressions are dramatic and exaggerated.
She is composed of circular shapes that you can squash and
stretch to animate her.

furious

fearful

joyful

greedy

scheming

conniving

JAFAR'S HEAD

The evil Jafar has a long, narrow face that always seems to be sneering.
Try to capture his cruel nature when drawing his face.

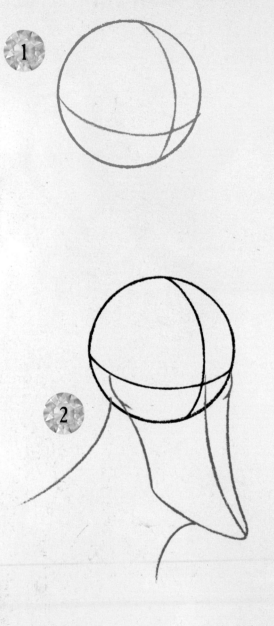

1

2

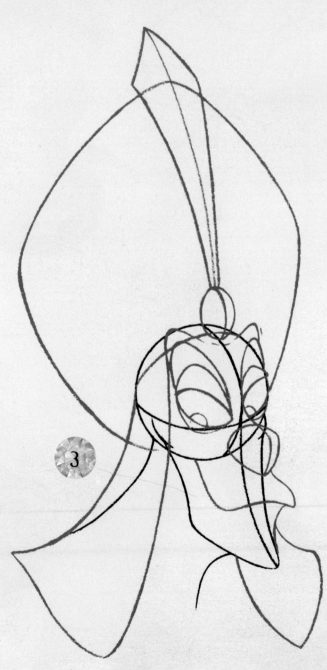

3

The ball of Jafar's head is small, with a long, angular jaw

turban has a
jewel in the
center

jewel detail

4

5

Jafar's Body

Jafar has broad, pointed shoulders that emphasize the length of his body and the wickedness of his character. Draw him with long lines and sharp angles.

4

5

turban detail

Jafar's Body

Jafar appears to be a wise counselor to the Sultan, but he really wants the throne for himself and wills all of his power to achieve it—until Aladdin gets in his way. Jafar is tall, thin, and stands above everyone. Remember to focus on the little details, such as his curlicue goatee and cobra-head staff.

1

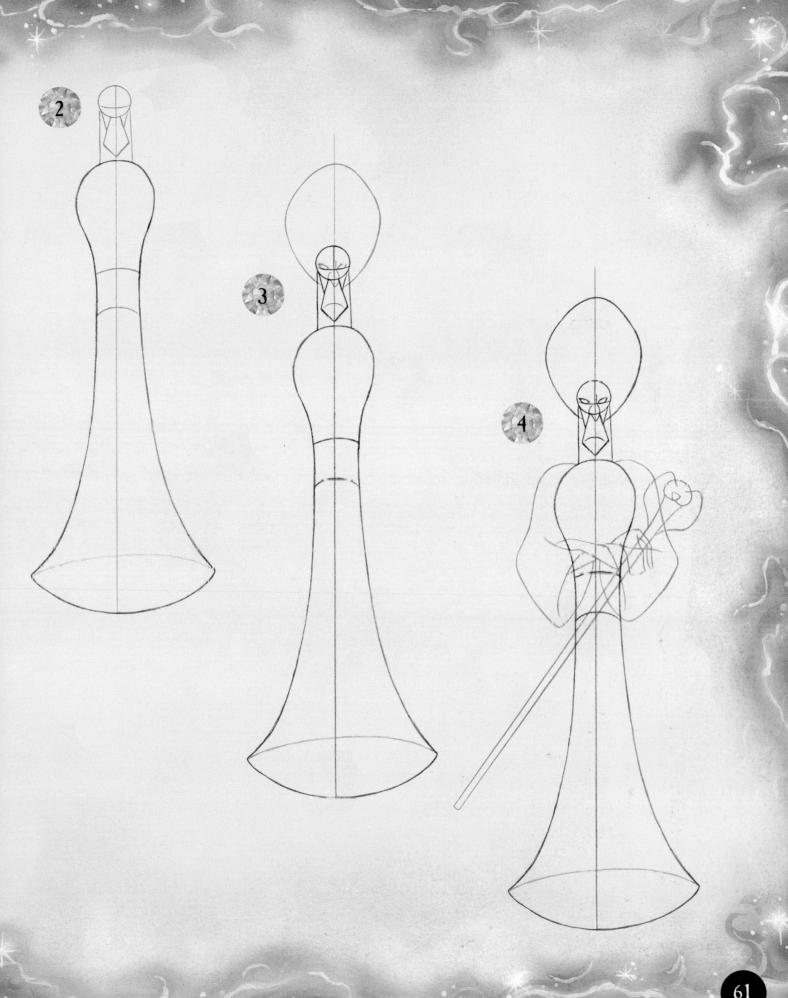

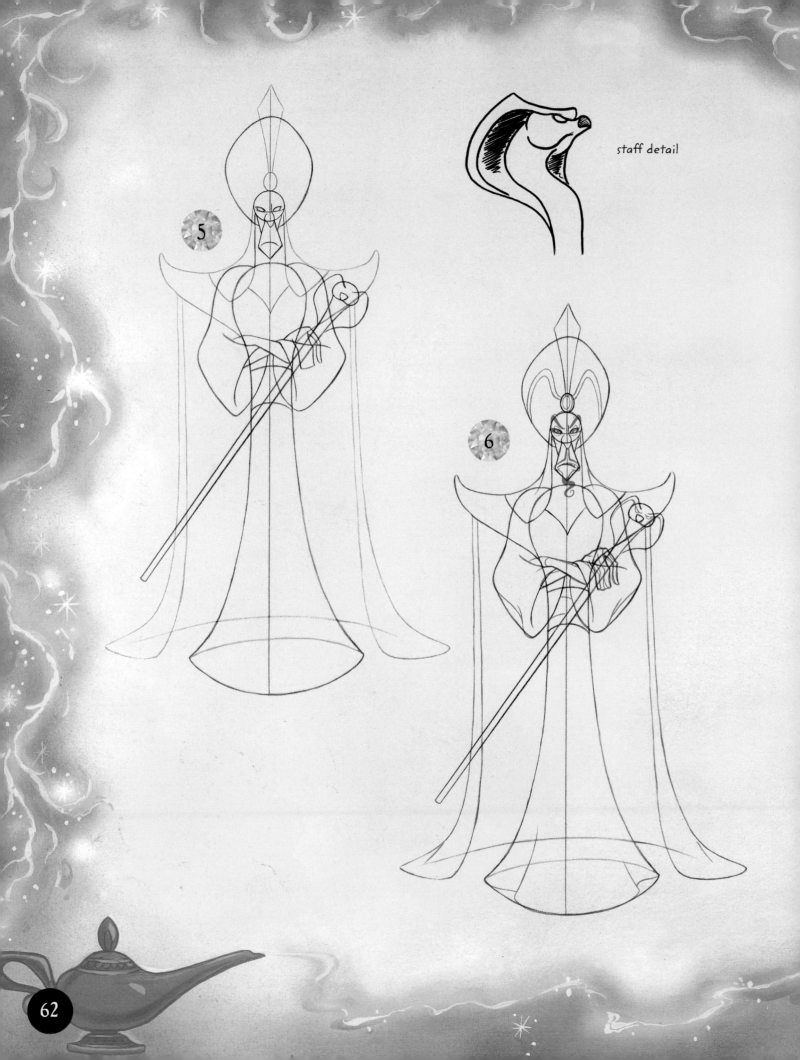

staff detail

5

6

Jafar and his cobra share the same icy glare—coincidence?

IAGO

Iago packs a lot of temper into his squat little body.
He is Jafar's volatile sidekick.

body is pear-shaped,
with a small ball for his
head

Iago

Iago is Jafar's squawking, magical sidekick, but it's hard to tell whose side he's really on. Sometimes, he does Jafar's dirty work; other times, he helps Jasmine out of a bind. Bottom line, he is a clever, sarcastic bird, always on the lookout for himself. Is he trustworthy? No! Is he funny? Yes!

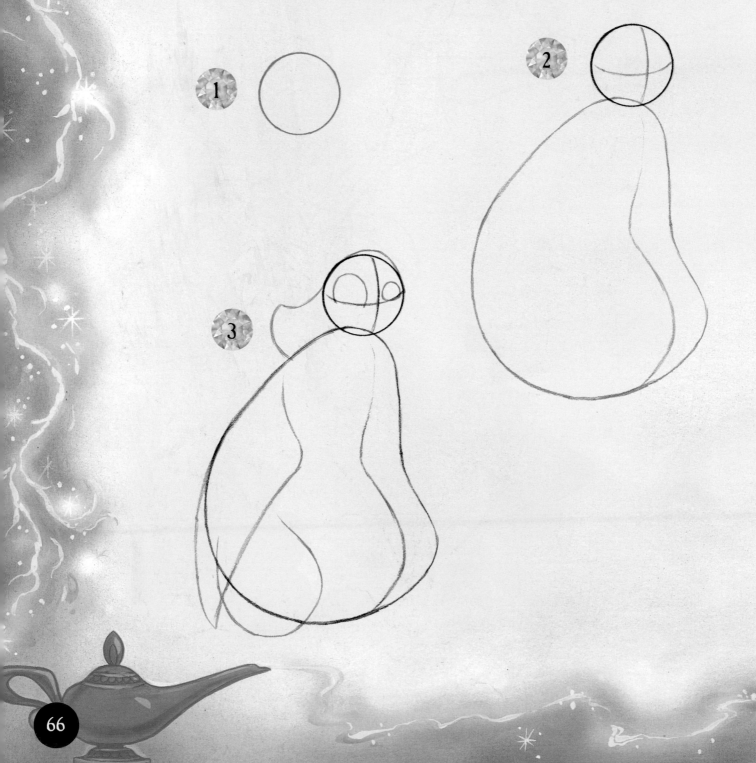

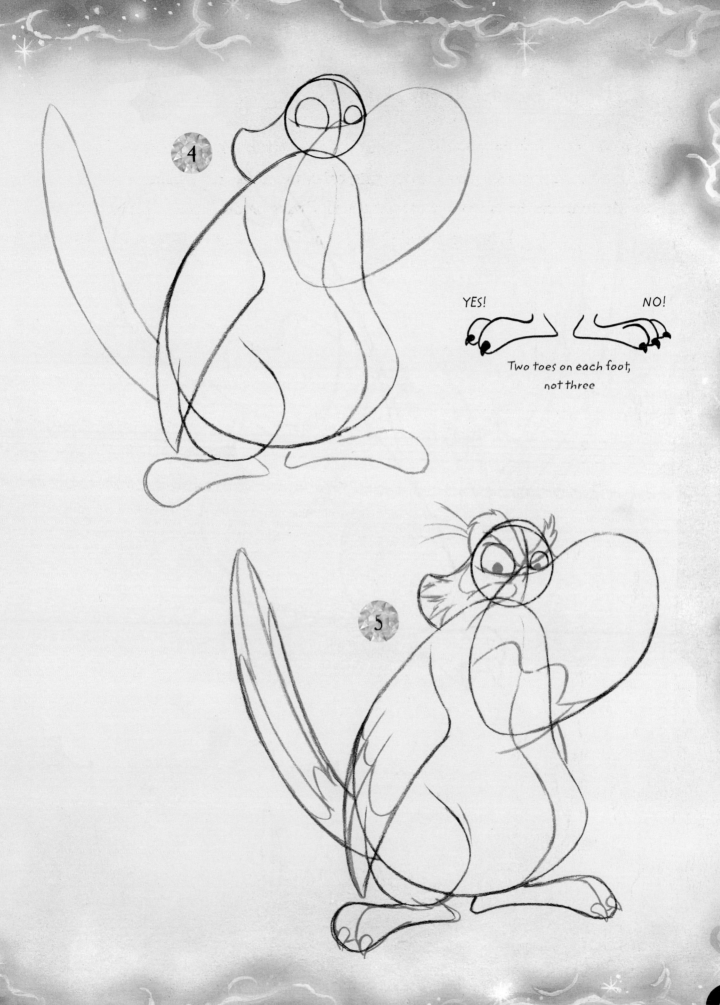

4

YES!

NO!

Two toes on each foot,
not three

5

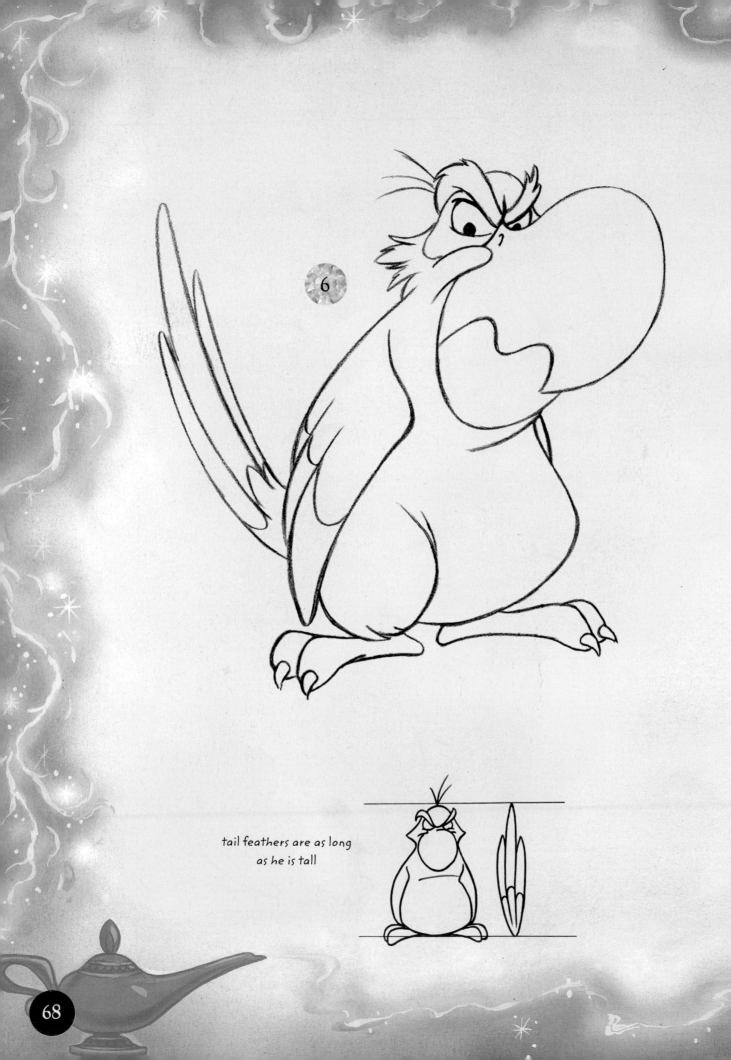

6

tail feathers are as long
as he is tall

THE QUEEN'S HEAD

The regal Queen is an aristocratic, strong-willed beauty.
But her diabolically evil nature clearly shows through in her expressions.

Notice how the angles that point downward— crown, headpiece, eyebrows, collar—convey an impression of evil

THE QUEEN'S BODY

In contrast to the Queen's sharp facial features,
her body consists of long, flowing curves.

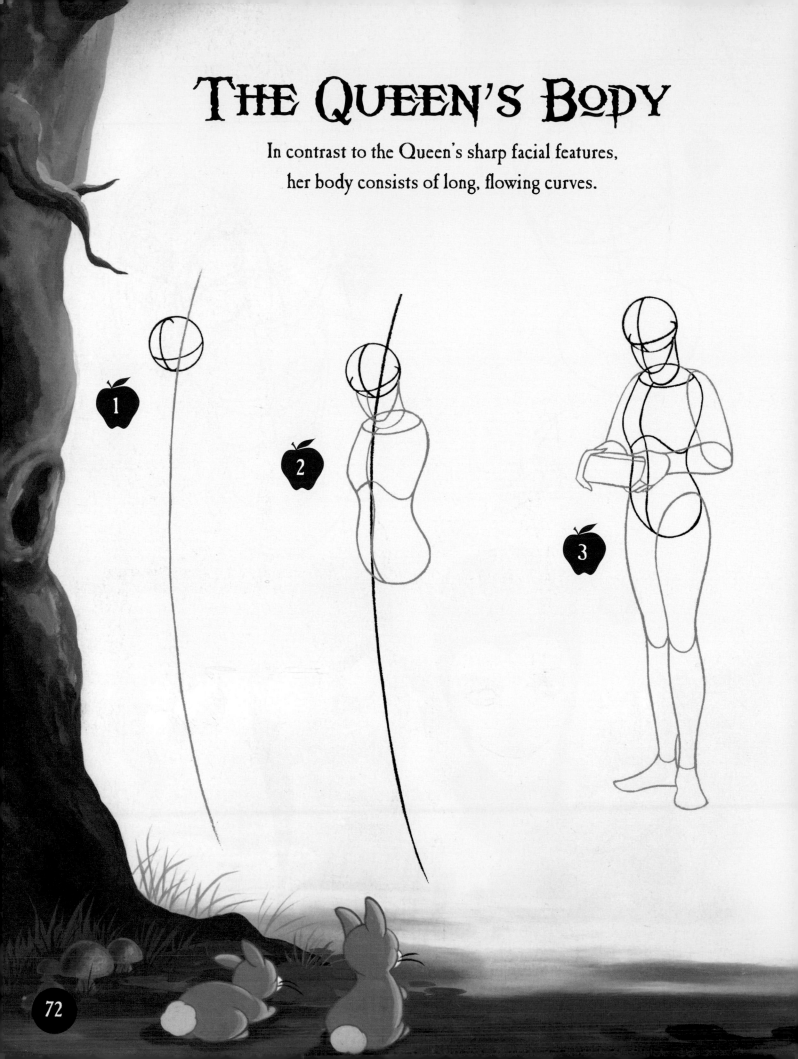

4

5

6

THE QUEEN'S BODY

Standing before the world, the Queen appears to be a regal beauty.
But at her core, she is an evil villain determined to destroy Snow White.

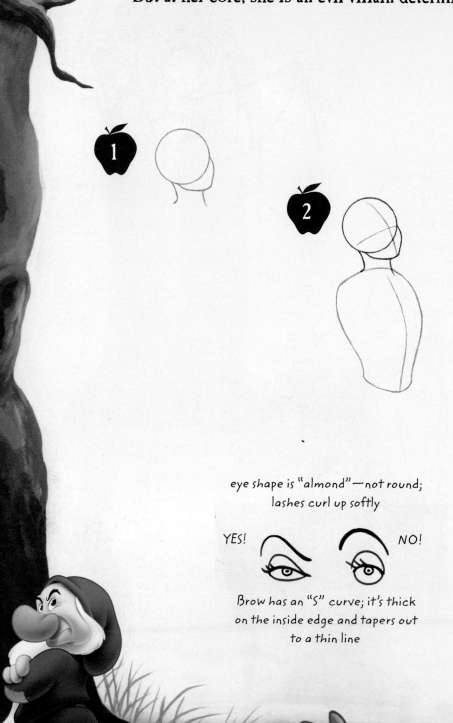

eye shape is "almond"—not round;
lashes curl up softly

YES!   NO!

Brow has an "S" curve; it's thick
on the inside edge and tapers out
to a thin line

4

YES!

NO!

Note the shape
of her lips

5

tassel detail

6

3/4 view

side view

brooch detail

NO!

YES!

The crown curves over her head and has a thicker edge on top and bottom

THE WITCH'S HEAD

When the evil Queen transforms herself to trick Snow White,
she reveals the true ugliness of her character.
Draw her with bulging eyes and a pointed chin.

THE WITCH'S BODY

The Witch's body is hunched forward and dressed in
ragged black clothing. Her hands are like claws.
As you practice drawing her, try to capture her wickedness.

The Witch's Body

The Witch uses her power to trick Snow White into taking a poison apple. Try to capture the Witch's evil look in your drawing, and don't forget to make that apple look tempting and delicious!

3

body is shaped
like a potato

she only has
one tooth

one brow is higher
than the other

brows are thick
and heavy

SCAR'S HEAD

The wicked Scar has a large nose and small eyes. His mane is darker and wilder than the other lions' manes, and his mouth curves in an evil grin.

④

⑤

Remember that Scar's scar
runs across his left eye

⑥

SCAR'S BODY

Scar has a long, lean body and large paws with the claws extended.
Can you capture some of his sinister nature in your drawing?

7

8

9

SCAR'S POSES AND EXPRESSIONS

Scar's rule devastates the Pride Lands and endangers the pride.

Here's how to draw him at his worst.

fierce

pleased

conniving

scary

THE HYENAS

The hyenas, Shenzi, Banzai, and Ed, prey upon
young Simba and Nala. Notice how their eyes give
away their individual personalities.

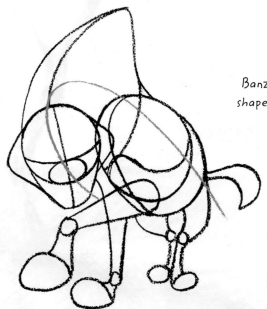

Banzai

*Banzai's eyes are two different
shapes—one is slightly narrowed*

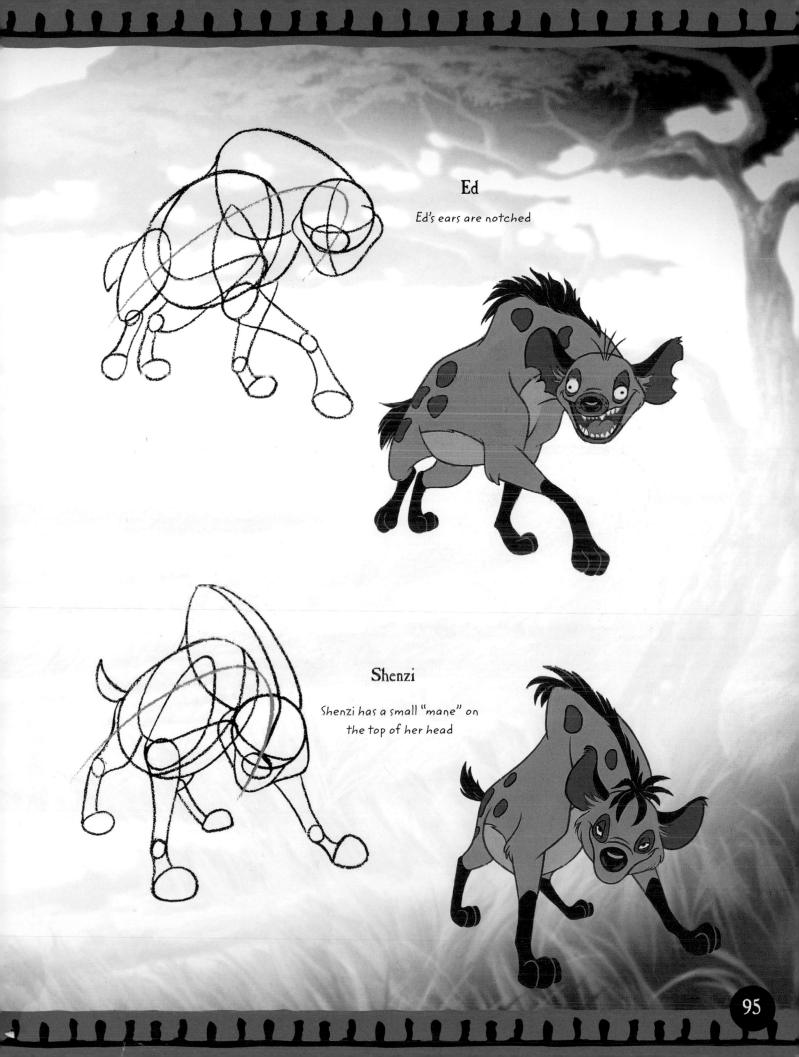

Ed

Ed's ears are notched

Shenzi

Shenzi has a small "mane" on the top of her head

Mother Gothel

Mother Gothel is young and beautiful—all because of Rapunzel's hair. Some might say that her beauty is not quite as spectacular as she believes. Remember that sometimes beauty is only skin deep, and Mother Gothel's wicked ways show her ugly side in her stance, her expressions, and her cruel comments.

4

5

features become more angular and textured when she is transformed into an old woman

6

Mother Gothel is more full-figured than Rapunzel, with wider hips and a broader torso

7

hair stays contained in
a bullet shape

Stabbington Brothers

The Stabbingtons are cutthroats of the worst kind.
Almost identical, one difference between them is that the
brother without the eye patch does all the talking.
But it's clear that they are more comfortable expressing
themselves with fists rather than with words.

1

2

3

hands are thick
and blocky

4

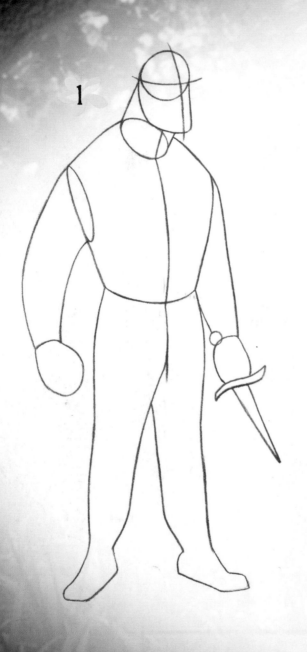

3

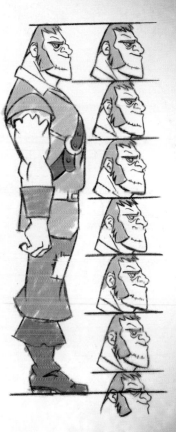

The Stabbingtons are about
6-1/3 heads high

4

Their faces are similar

5

Dr. Facilier

Dr. Facilier is a sinister and charismatic man of dark magic who works in the French Quarter. He lures unsuspecting passersby into deals where he promises to give them their heart's desire in return for money. However, when fulfilling those promises, Facilier uses dark magic for his own personal gain. Facilier yearns to expand his small-time business so he can spread darkness and corruption throughout New Orleans... and become fantastically wealthy in the process.

hat is a tall cylinder

slight flair on top

he has a feather in his hat

short brim

2

3

YES! **Ear shape is more angular**   NO! **Too round**

4

 YES! Moustache is pencil thin

NO! Not too large

profile

spats cover
his shoes

Lawrence

Lawrence is Naveen's stiff, pompous, roly-poly valet. Though he plays the part of the prince's dutiful manservant, Lawrence is secretly envious of the Prince's charm, good looks, and position.

nose is round
and upturned

YES!   NO!   NO!

1

body is
pear-
shaped

mouth sits low
on the face

large
lower
lip

5

115

Zurg

The Universe—and Al's Toy Barn—is not safe with the evil Emperor Zurg on the loose. Zurg is smart enough to escape from the store and strong enough to take on Buzz and New Buzz, but he's unlucky enough to be on the receiving end of Rex's swinging tail.

hands are composed of sharp steel parts with claw-like fingers

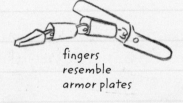

fingers resemble armor plates

5 torso rings

STEP 1

angle of horns is about 45 degrees

YES!

NO!

NO!

concave   convex

Zurg's gauntlet

Buzz's gauntlet

"Feet" are 3 wheels

visor appears triangular in all views

116

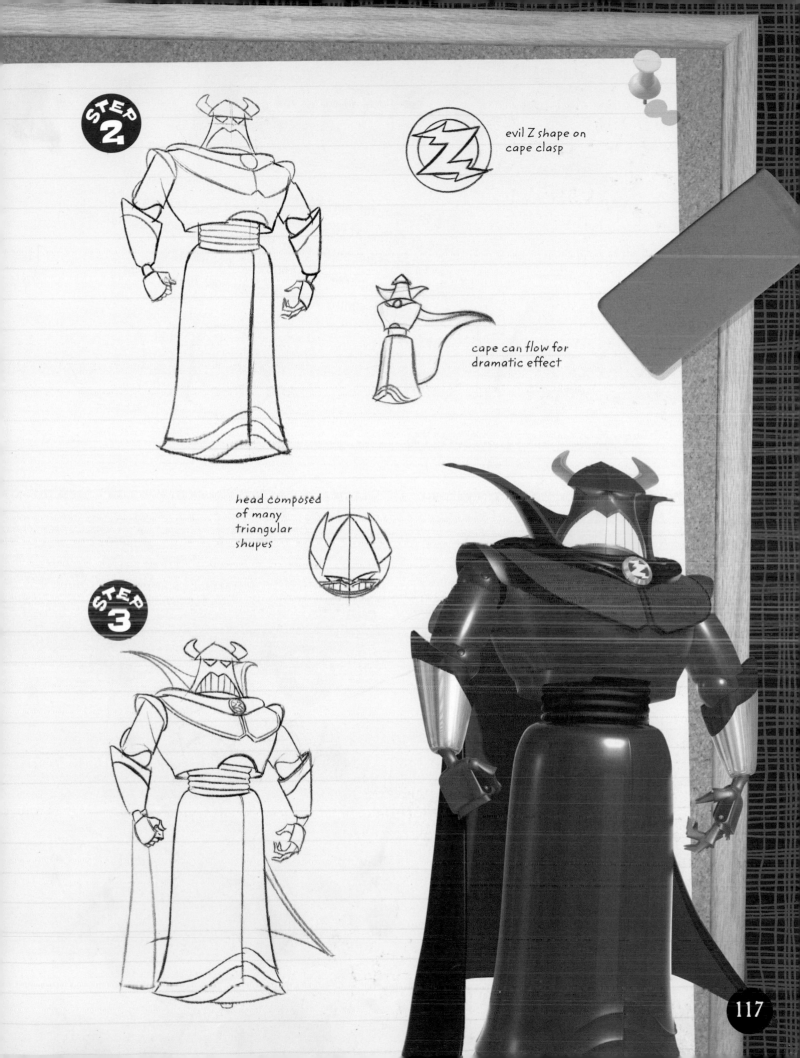

STEP 2

evil Z shape on cape clasp

cape can flow for dramatic effect

head composed of many triangular shapes

STEP 3

THE PROSPECTOR

The Prospector may seem like a nice grandfatherly type of fellow at first, but when his true feelings are revealed, it becomes clear that he's just plain selfish and mean. Having never belonged to a child, the Prospector simply doesn't know how to play—or be loved.

head is bell-shaped

STEP 1

moustache changes with mood

beard, brows, and moustache are loose and bushy

relaxed gesture

stretch

body like a half-filled flour sack

squish

excited gesture

STEP 2

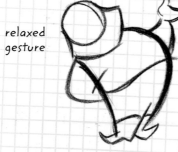

STEP 3

The Prospector is never without his pickaxe

boot flares at top

hat curls up in front and back

pointy beard in side view

button detail

small hands with slender fingers

tight-fitting sleeves

119

LOTSO

In *Toy Story 3*, Lots-o'-Huggin' Bear—a.k.a Lotso—seems like nothing more than the nicest teddy bear at Sunnyside Daycare. But Lotso's true colors are exposed when he traps Andy's toys in the Caterpillar Room with all of the rambunctious toddlers—and later when he leaves the toys to be incinerated at the garbage dump.

STEP 1

teardrop-shaped paws

nose is an upside-down rounded triangle

eyebrows are
wide and bushy

YES!

NO!

ears are two
half circles

STEP
2

eyes are round and set close together

STEP 3

3

His cane is
a wooden
mallet

CHUNK

One of Lotso's cronies at Sunnyside Daycare, Chunk, is a two-faced plastic rock monster who goes from friendly to foul with the punch of a button.

STEP 1

STEP 2

STEP 3

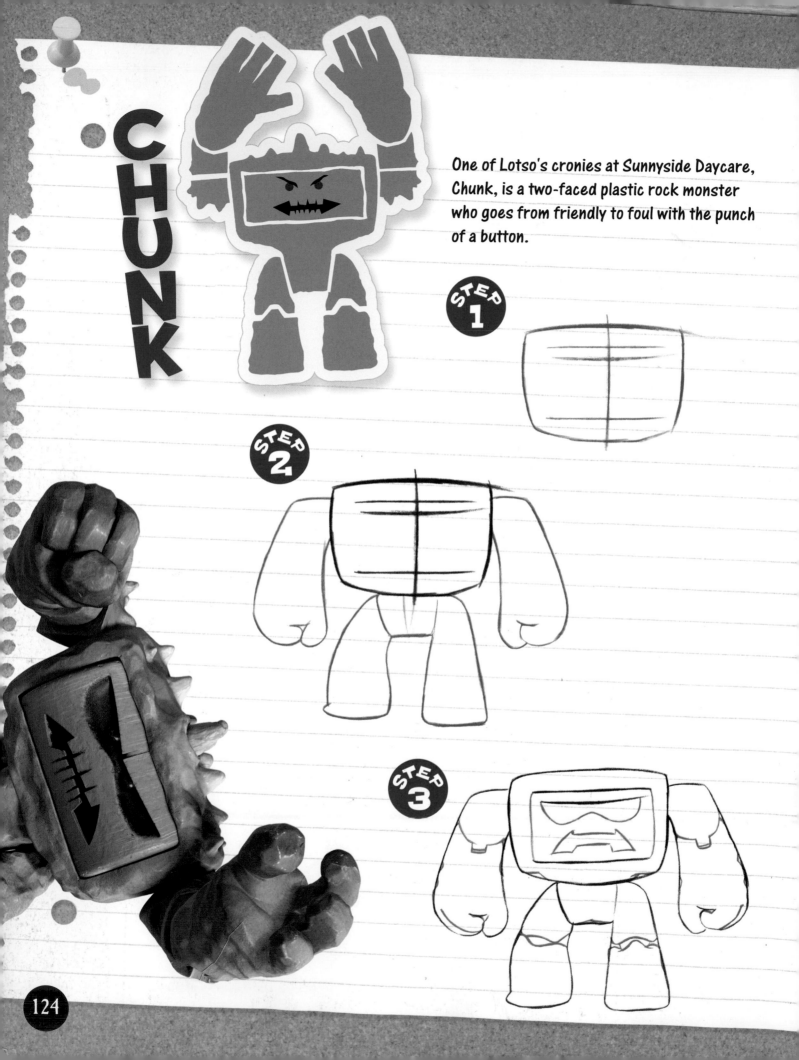

STEP 4

Chunk has two faces

TWITCH

Twitch is the tough, muscular, staff-wielding, insect-headed member of Lotso's gang at Sunnyside Daycare. He doesn't say much, but he's not a bug any of Andy's toys want to mess with.

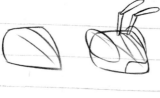

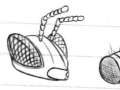

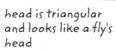

head is triangular and looks like a fly's head

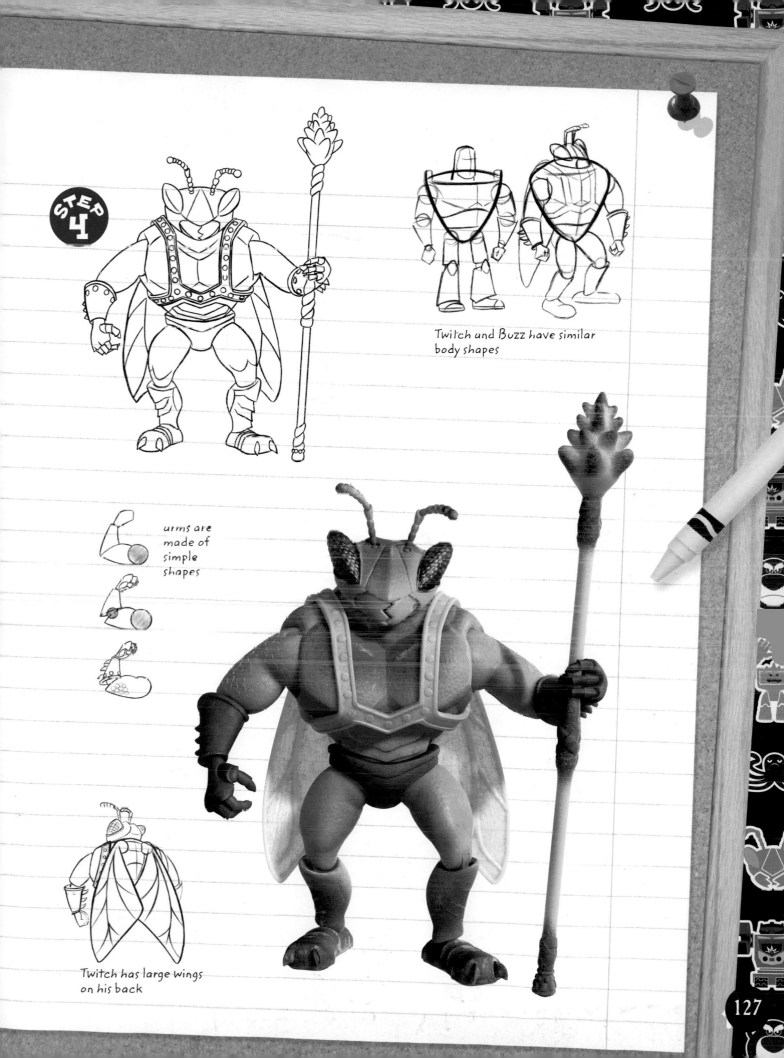

STEP 4

Twitch and Buzz have similar body shapes

arms are made of simple shapes

Twitch has large wings on his back

Chick

Chick is a racing veteran with a chip on his shoulder. He's a ruthless competitor who is notorious for cheating his way to second place. Always a runner-up, he'll do anything to win.

STEP 1

YES!

tires are big and wide

NO!

not too thin

STEP 2

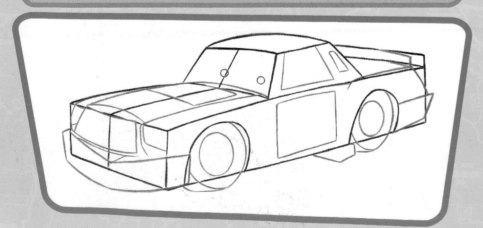

FOR OLDER ACTIVE CARS

STEP 3

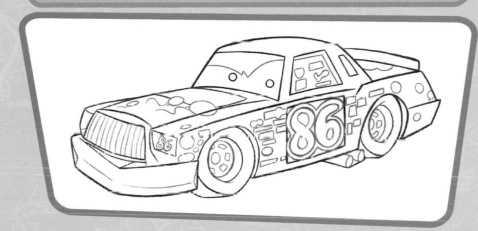

YES!

NO!

Chick has beady
pupils and a sharp
peak between his eyes

Chick considers himself prime
real estate and is covered with
sponsor stickers—so get creative
with sticker shapes and placement

STEP 4

Professor Z

The smart and savvy mad scientist Professor Z has mastered the art of sophisticated weapons design and has created an elaborate device disguised as a camera that can harm cars without leaving a trace of evidence. His goal is to sabotage the World Grand Prix racers. Will he succeed?

his broken roof rack gives the appearance of a hair comb-over

Step 1

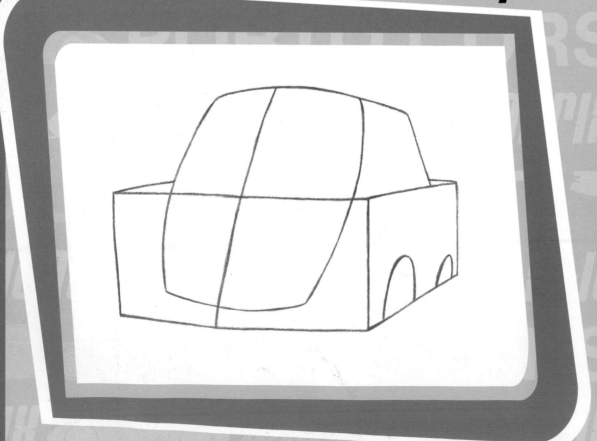

Step 2

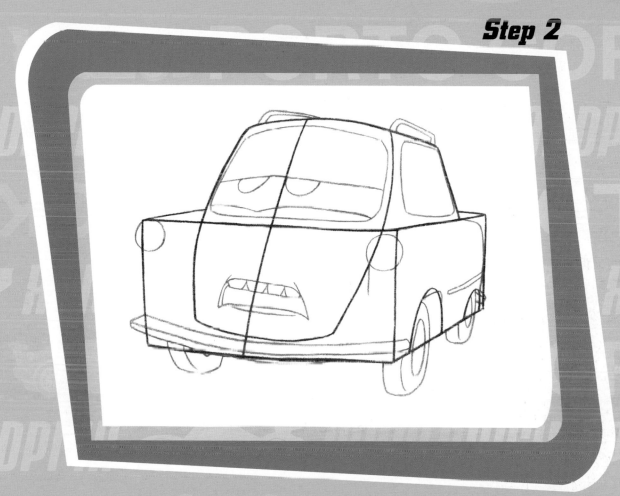

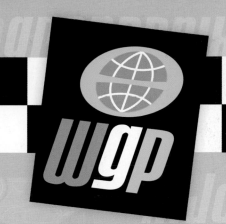

Professor Z looks the same coming or going!

Professor Z is really small

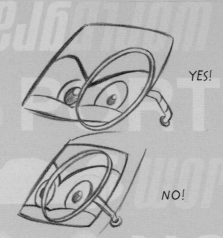

YES!

NO!

be careful when posing
Professor Z that his body
angle doesn't cause his
eye to be cut across by
his monocle

Step 3

Step 4

Grem

Grem is another of Professor Z's goons. Grem and his partner-in-crime, Acer, don't have the fancy gadgets that the spy cars have. But they are tough and relentless. They'll do anything to stop the secret agents!

Step 1

Grem has a distinctive decal on his side that resembles a hockey stick

Step 2

draw lower eyelids to make his expressions more shifty

from behind, his body shape looks like an upside-down cup on a saucer

Step 3

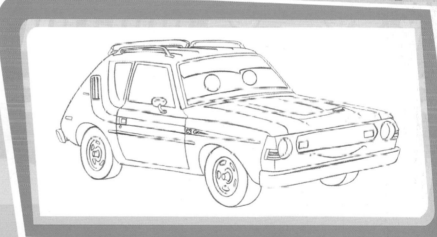

his front grille looks like a moustache, and he's missing some teeth because he's been in some fights

Step 4

when they're doing their dirty work, Grem and Acer are in contact with their boss by wearing headsets

Acer

Acer is one of Professor Z's main goons who carries out all of his dirty work. This Lemon, along with his buddy Grem, enjoys taking out the World Grand Prix racers one by one by aiming the TV camera device at them while they're zooming down the racetrack.

Step 1

NO! not too short

YES! Acer has a tall cab

Step 2

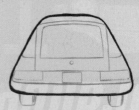

keep body shape simple, boxy, and soft

Step 3

Grem and Acer are roughly the same size

Step 4

Miles Axlerod

Sir Miles Axlerod has devoted his life and fortune—acquired as an oil baron—to creating a renewable, alternative fuel called Allinol, which he showcases at a three-country race called the World Grand Prix. But Mater and his friends soon discover that Allinol isn't all it's cracked up to be—and neither is Axlerod.

Step 1

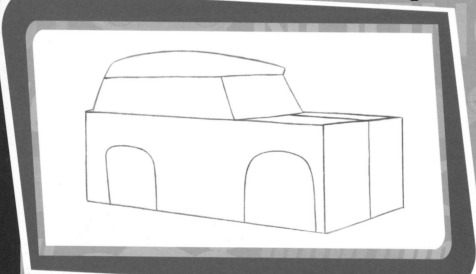

he has a very boxy appearance from the front

Step 2

Step 3

a winch on the back
carries his electrical plug

Step 4

the top of his cab should
resemble an English
driving cap

AUTOPILOT

In *Wall•E*, the autopilot, nicknamed Auto, has complete control over the *Axiom*. Shaped like a ship's wheel with a large eye in its center, Auto is attached to a long, electronic neck device that allows him to maneuver around the ship's bridge. He steers the *Axiom* and looks out the windows into space with his big eye, but he's not as innocent as he seems. When his real (and very evil) directive is discovered, he uses his robotic "finger" device not only to push buttons but also to poke the Captain in the eye!

Autopilot resembles an old ship's wheel

STEP 1

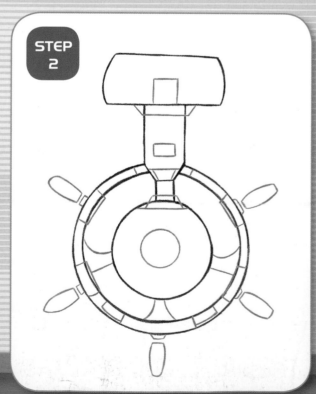

STEP 2

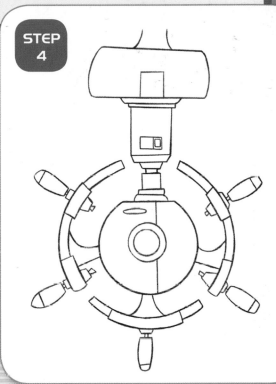

STEP 4

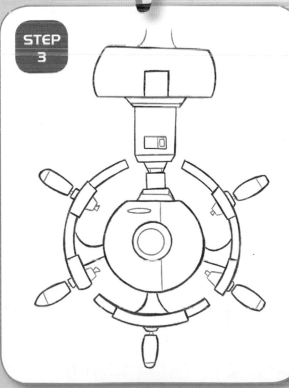

STEP 3

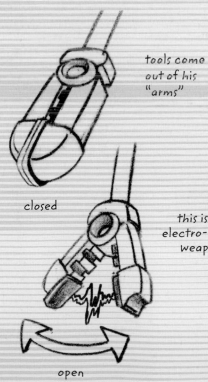

tools come out of his "arms"

closed

this is an electro-shock weapon

open

GO-4

light inside head flashes in an emergency

GO-4 is a robot that is supposed to serve the Captain and Auto, all for the good of the *Axiom* and its passengers. But once Auto is given his secret directive (never to steer the ship back to Earth), GO-4 becomes Auto's minion. With a siren on his head, GO-4 doesn't hesitate to declare an emergency to try to stop WALL•E and EVE—or anyone else who might try to help send the *Axiom* back to Earth.

STEP 1

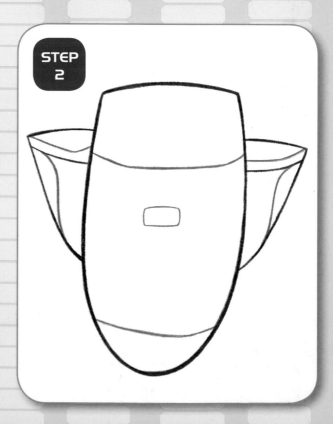

STEP 2

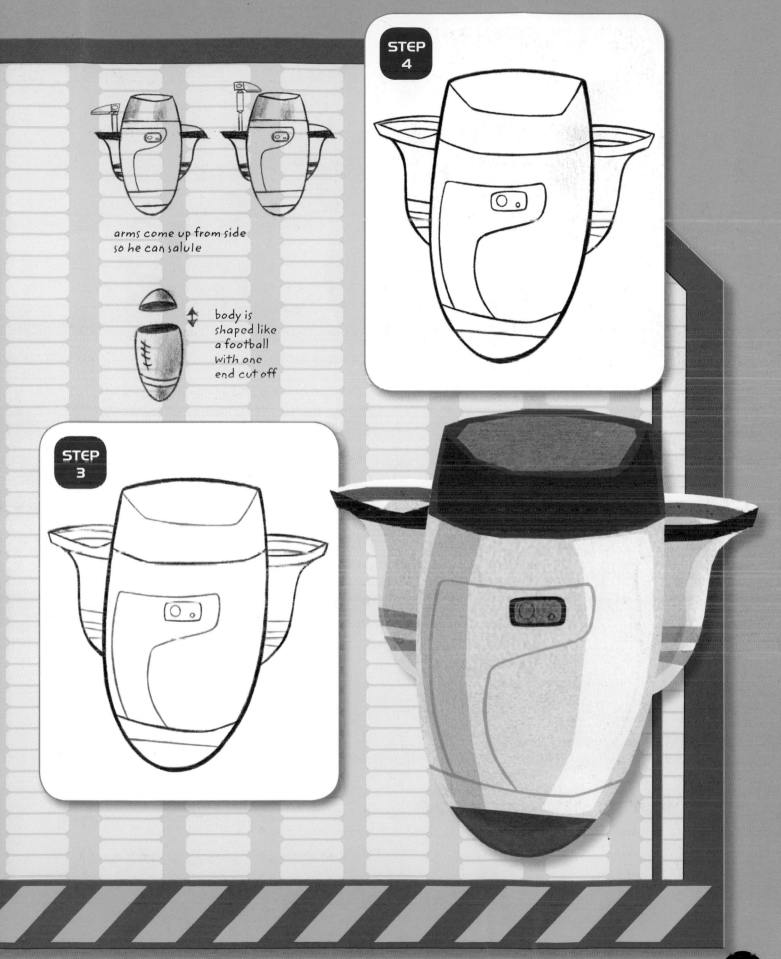

arms come up from side
so he can salute

body is
shaped like
a football
with one
end cut off

STEP 3

STEP 4